GATE GUARDS

GATE GUARDS

Philip Chinnery

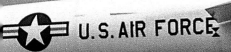

Airlife
England

First published 1988
by Airlife Publishing Ltd.

ISBN 1 85310 043 9 Case Bound
ISBN 1 85310 042 0 Paperback

Printed in Singapore by Kyodo-Shing Loong Printing Inds PTE Ltd.

Airlife Publishing Ltd.

7 St. John's Hill, Shrewsbury, England.

INTRODUCTION

Where did they go? North American built thousands of F-86 Sabres, Boeing built nearly 900 C-97 Stratofreighters and tankers, Grumman produced thousands of S-2 Trackers and so the list goes on. Where are they all now? Scrapped mostly, or in storage awaiting disposal.

Over the last twenty years responsible authorities have gradually woken up to the fact that examples of these aircraft should be preserved. For many types, it is too late — few examples remain of the Savage, the Banshee or the Javelin, to name but a few.

Traditionally, museums have been the repositories for old aircraft worthy of preservation, but most have space limitations and must pick and choose which types to display. Fortunately, particularly in the United States where the Air Force Heritage Programme is underway, the business of preserving old aircraft is well in hand.

Not often seen by the public, Grumman F-11B Tiger *138647* is preserved at the Naval Weapons Centre at China Lake in California. *(Author)*

There can be few air bases this side of the Iron Curtain that do not possess a gate guard — an old aircraft, usually positioned near the base entrance, in varying conditions of repair and often 'up a pole'. The latter being an attempt to portray the aircraft in its normal flying attitude and often limited only by the imagination of the people responsible for the display. In the case of the B-47 and B-52 preserved at the Oklahoma City State Fair Grounds, or some of the aircraft preserved in Pakistan, some people are more imaginative than others.

McDonnell F-101B Voodoo *57-0438* preserved outside the Gulf Coast Community College at Panama City in Florida. 480 F-101Bs were built and were capable of launching two Genie nuclear missiles. *(Chris Allen)*

The United States clearly leads the field where the preservation of old aircraft is concerned. Very often there is more than one gate guard at each air base and it is becoming popular now for bases to have their own out-of-doors aircraft collection as well. Perhaps the Americans have an advantage in that they have many more aircraft to chose from. Nowadays, when a type is withdrawn from service there is usually enough of them for one to be made available to half the air bases in the country.

The gate guard situation in countries outside the United States and Great Britain is varied. For obvious reasons it has proven impossible to visit, photograph and assess the gate guards at bases in every country in the world. Hopefully, globe-trotting readers may well bear in mind the possibility of a second gate guards book in the future and think twice before passing up the opportunity of photographing gate guards in Africa, the Far East or anywhere east of the Berlin Wall. For the moment, we have a P-47 Thunderbolt gate guard in Brazil, a nice Mustang at Basa air base in the Philippines and plenty of the author's favourite, the F-86 Sabre, including some from Japan.

One problem that the author did encounter was that nowadays some gate guards appear to be more mobile than others. The fact that one aircraft may be on the gate of a certain air base this week, is no guarantee that it will still be there next week. It is therefore not recommended that one travels to an air base with the express intention of photographing a particular aircraft. One could find that it is now on the gate of a base on the other side of the country.

North American F-100D Super Sabre *54-2294* on the main gate at Homestead AFB, Florida wearing the fin markings of the 31st Tactical Fighter Wing. *(Author's Collection)*

De Havilland Vampire T.11 *XD429* at the Royal Air Force College, Cranwell. Correct serial number is *XD542/7604M.*
(Jim Simpson Collection)

Some of the aircraft colour schemes and serial numbers are also rather dubious. The Luftwaffe has on more than one occasion put an aircraft on display wearing a serial number which is actually the postal code of the air base! Tracing the ancestry of some gate guards is no mean task, although the situation concerning Royal Air Force gate guards is well in hand.

Many of the photographs in this book are from Jim Simpson's extensive gate guard collection. Jim is currently working on a book of Royal Air Force gate guards and the final work is awaited with interest. Graham Robson and Chris Allen both kindly dug through their large collections of United States gate guards pictures and together with Jim, their pictures form the bulk of the book. Chris Pocock, Paul Jackson, Peter Foster and Lindsay Peacock must also be thanked for the loan of rare pictures from their collections. The author sincerely hopes that the reader will appreciate the final product.

Vought A-7E Corsair II *156815,* in the markings of USS Midway NF: 001 on the gate of Lemoore Naval Air Station in California.
(Jim Simpson Collection)

Philip D. Chinnery
Hayes, Middlesex, March 1988

Opposite: Royal Australian Navy Firefly AS.6 *WB518* on display at the War Memorial at Griffith, New South Wales.
(Jim Simpson Collection)

Opposite: Royal Australian Air Force North American Sabre Mk.31 *A94-942* on display at No.1 Central Ammunition Depot at Kingswood, New South Wales. *(Jim Simpson Collection)*

Below: Royal Australian Air Force Lockheed SP-2H Neptune *A89-275* at the Royal Australian Air Force Museum, Point Cook, Victoria. *(Author's Collection)*

Opposite: Royal Australian Navy De Havilland Sea Venom
FAW.53 *WZ943* on display in Kalander Street, Nowra, New South
Wales. *(Author's Collection)*

Below: Belgian Air Force Gloster Meteor F.8 *EG-79* on the gate
at Brustem Air Base. *(Jim Simpson Collection)*

Opposite: Brazilian Navy Lockheed P-15 Neptune *7009* at Salvador Air Base wearing the red griffin badge of 1 Squadron, 7 Group, Coastal Command. *(Jim Simpson Collection)*

Below: Belgian Air Force Hawker Hunter F.4 *ID-123*, the gate guard at Koksijde Air Base. *(Author's Collection)*

Opposite: Brazilian Air Force Republic P-47D Thunderbolt
419660 on the gate at Santa Cruz Air Base in wartime markings.
(Jim Simpson Collection)

Below: Belgian Air Force Republic RF-84F Thunderflash *FR-32*
preserved at Bierset Air Base. *(Jim Simpson Collection)*

Opposite: Royal Canadian Air Force Canadair CL-13 Sabre Mk.1 *19101* preserved at the Canadian Forces Base, Edmonton. *(Author's Collection)*

Below: Royal Canadian Navy McDonnell F2H-3 Banshee *126402*, one of 39 transferred from the US Navy in 1955. Part of the collection at Canadian Forces Base, Shearwater. *(Paul Jackson)*

Opposite: Royal Canadian Navy North American AT-6 Harvard
2777 preserved at Shearwater. *(Paul Jackson)*

Below: Royal Canadian Air Force Avro-Canada CF-100 *18626* in
433 Squadron markings on display at North Bay, Ontario.
(Jim Simpson Collection)

Opposite: Royal Canadian Navy Sikorsky HO4S Chickasaw *891* at Shearwater. *(Paul Jackson)*

Below: Royal Canadian Navy Grumman CS2F (CP-121) Tracker *1501* at the Canadian Forces Base at Shearwater, Nova Scotia. *(Paul Jackson)*

Opposite: Royal Canadian Navy General Motors TBM-3 Avenger *85861* at the Canadian Forces Base at Shearwater, Nova Scotia.
(Paul Jackson)

Below: Wearing Canadian Armed Force/Navy markings, Canadair CT-133 Silver Star *133038* preserved at Shearwater.
(Author's Collection)

Opposite: Canadair CT-133 Silver Star *133181* and Canadair CF-104 Starfighter *12872* at Canadian Forces Base Cold Lake.
(Jim Simpson Collection)

Below: Royal Canadian Air Force Canadair CT-133 Silver Star *21533* in 408 Squadron markings at Edmonton-Namao in Alberta.
(Author's Collection)

Opposite: French Air Force Dassault Mystere IVA *120* displayed on the gate at Cazuax in the markings 8-NE of 8 Squadron. *(Author's Collection)*

Below: Royal Danish Air Force North American TF-100F Sabre *GT-949* preserved at Karup Air Base. *(Jim Simpson Collection)*

Opposite: Dassault Mirage 111-T *01* is preserved on the gate of the Armee de l'Air technical training school at Rochefort/St. Agnant. *(Jim Simpson Collection)*

Below: French Air Force Mirage 111RD *361*, fitted with a Mirage 111A nose, preserved outside the operations building at Strasburg/Entzheim. *(Jim Simpson Collection)*

Overleaf: Luftwaffe Fokker-built RF-104G Starfighter *25+07* painted as 80+58, guards the disused airfield at Erding. *(Author's Collection)*

Opposite: French Air Force Marcel Dassault MD450 Ouragan *187/U1,* preserved at Tours — St. Symphorien. *(Jim Simpson Collection)*

Below: Luftwaffe Canadair CL-13B Sabre Mk.6 *JB+114* preserved at Jever as *BB+103* (a Mk.5). *(Author's Collection)*

Opposite: On display at Lahr, West Germany is Royal Canadian
Air Force Canadair CL-13B Sabre Mk6 *23444*. *(Paul Jackson)*

Below: Bundesmarine Armstrong-Whitworth Sea Hawk F.101
RB+363 preserved at Eggebek in the markings of Marinef-
liegergeschwader 2 (MFG2). *(Jim Simpson Collection)*

Opposite: Luftwaffe Republic RF-84F Thunderflash *BD-119* displayed in the markings of Reconnaissance Wing Aufklarungsgeschwader 51 (AKG51) 'Immelmann', at Osnabruck. *(Jim Simpson Collection)*

Below: Royal Canadian Air Force Avro-Canada CF-100 Canuck *100784* on display at the Canadian base at Sollingen, West Germany. *(Paul Jackson)*

Opposite: Canadair Lockheed CF-104G Starfighter *12785*, one of the four gate guards at the Canadian base at Sollingen, West Germany. *(Jim Simpson Collection)*

Below left: Italian Air Force Republic F-84F Thunderstreak *MM53-6845* at Rivolto, wearing the colours of the Diavoli Rossi aerobatic display team. *(Jim Simpson Collection)*

Bottom left: Also on display at Rivolto, North American F-86E Sabre *MM19685* 4-20 in the colours of the Cavallino Rampante aerobatic display team. *(Jim Simpson Collection)*

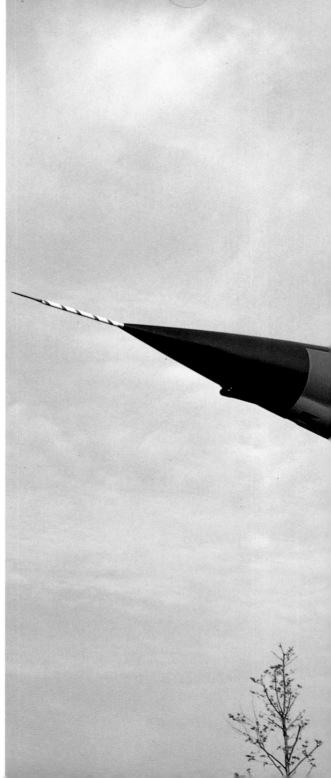

Opposite: Also preserved at Sollingen in West Germany is Royal
Canadian Air Force Canadair CL-13B Sabre Mk.6 *23605*.
(Paul Jackson)

Below: Japanese Air Self Defence Force Lockheed T-33A *51-
5629* at Hyakuri Air Base in the markings of 301 Hikotai
(Squadron). *(Author's Collection)*

Opposite: Also on display at Hyakuri Air Base, North American F-86F Sabre *92-7885* in 9 Hikotai (Squadron) markings. *(Author's Collection)*

Below: One of a large number of North American F-86D Sabres on display in Japan, *04-8187* is preserved at Nyutabaru Air Base in 202 Hikotai (Squadron) markings. *(Author's Collection)*

Opposite: North American T-6G *52-0022* is only one of half a dozen former Japanese Self Defence Force aircraft preserved at Iruma Air Base. *(Author's Collection)*

Below: Another of the aircraft on display at Nyutabaru is Lockheed F-104J Starfighter *46-8656*, marked as *36-8535* of 204 Hikotai. *(Peter Foster)*

Opposite: An impressive gate guard at Tsuiki Air Base, North American F-86F Sabre *92-7938* wears the markings of 6 Hikotai (Squadron). *(Peter Foster)*

Below left: North American F-86F Sabre *82-7778* preserved at Komaki Air Base. *(Author's Collection)*

Bottom left: Royal Malaysian Air Force Canadair CL-41G Tebuan preserved behind the Ministry of Defence in Kuala Lumpur and wearing construction number 22-05. *(Chris Pocock)*

Opposite: Preserved at Eindhoven, Republic F-84F Thunder-streak *P-231* wears the golden Centaur badge of 314 Squadron, Royal Netherlands Air Force. *(Jim Simpson Collection)*

Below: North American F-86K Sabre *Q-283* on display outside Twenthe Air Base wearing the black Panther badge of 500 Squadron. *(Author's Collection)*

Opposite: Japanese Air Self Defence Force Lockheed F-104J Starfighter *36-8544* on display at Naha Air Base wearing 207 Hikotai (Squadron) colours. *(Author's Collection)*

Below left: Fokker-built Hawker Hunter F.4 N-122 guards the gate at Soesterberg Air Base wearing the black Scorpion badge of 325 Squadron. *(Jim Simpson Collection)*

Bottom left: North American F-86K Sabre *41290* at Gardermoen Air Base, is only one of six owned by the Royal Norwegian Air Force Collection. *(Jim Simpson Collection)*

Opposite: Part of the Royal Norwegian Air Force collection, Supermarine Spitfire PR.XI *PL979* resides at Gardermoen Air Base, some 55 kilometres north-west of Oslo. *(Author's Collection)*

Below: Wearing colourful day-glow markings and the squadron code DP-K, Lockheed T-33A *117546* is also preserved at 'Flymuseet 2062' at Gardermoen Air Base. *(Author's Collection)*

Opposite: The award for the most precariously displayed gate guard in the book, must go to this Pakistan Air Force Lockheed F-104A Starfighter *56-0879* at Masroor Air Base. *(Lindsay Peacock)*

Below: One of only 26 Lockheed F-104B Starfighters built, *57-1309* guards the gate at the Pakistan Air Force training base at Risalpur. *(Lindsay Peacock)*

Opposite: Another well preserved resident of Gardermoen Air Base, Republic F-84G Thunderjet *51-11209* wearing squadron markings from three decades in the past. *(Author's Collection)*

Below: Another Gardermoen resident, this Republic RF-84F Thunderflash carries the serial number *51-17053* and the squadron code AZ-G. *(Author's Collection)*

Opposite: North American AT-6 Harvard *T4246* on display at Risalpur Air Base. *(Lindsay Peacock)*

Below: North American F-86F Sabre *51-13447*, an impressive gate guard at Sargodha Air Base. *(Lindsay Peacock)*

Opposite: Another North American F-86F Sabre, *53-1176,* on display at the Pakistan Air Force Base at Korangi Creek. *(Lindsay Peacock)*

Below: Pakistan Air Force North American F-86F Sabre *55-5005* preserved at Peshawar Air Base. *(Lindsay Peacock)*

Opposite: Wearing very colourful, but weathered markings,
North American P-51D Mustang *3733* guarding the gate at Basa
Air Base. *(Chris Pocock)*

Below: Philippine Air Force North American F-86D Sabre *18436,*
preserved at Basa Air Base. *(Chris Pocock)*

Opposite: Portuguese Air Force North American F-86F Sabre
5301 on the gate at Monte Real Air Base. *(Author's Collection)*

Below: North American F-86F Sabre *24428* 'Budjak', one of half a
dozen aircraft preserved on the gate of Basa Air Base.
(Author's Collection)

Opposite: Republic of Korea Air Force Douglas B-26K Invader *64-17651* is one of a dozen aircraft on display at the Korean War Memorial in Seoul. *(Peter Foster)*

Below: In storage for the Musee do Ar at Sintra, Lockheed P2V-5 Neptune *4711* was one of a dozen transferred to Portugal from the Dutch Navy. *(Author's Collection)*

Opposite: Spanish Air Force North American F-86F Sabre *C5-70* preserved inside Zaragoza Air Base, wearing the tiger badge of number 11 Fighter Wing. *(Chris Pocock)*

Below: Swedish Air Force Saab J-35D Draken guarding the gate at Uppsala Air Base. *(Chris Pocock)*

Opposite: Convair PBY-5A Canso *47001* at the Swedish Air Force Museum at Malmslätt. Note Percival Pembroke and Vickers Varsity in the background. *(Author's Collection)*

Below: Royal Thai Air Force North American F-86F Sabre *5022* preserved at the Air Force Academy, Don Muang Air Base, Bangkok. *(Chris Pocock)*

Opposite: De Havilland Sea Vixen FAW.2 *XJ580* in the markings of E:131 of 899 Naval Air Squadron outside Queensway's, Wilverley Road, Portsmouth. *(Jim Simpson Collection)*

Below: The prototype Pilatus P.2 *U-101* outside the Pilatus factory at Stans. The Swiss Air Force withdrew the last of these trainers from service in 1980 *(Paul Jackson)*

Opposite: Hawker Hunter F.51 *XF979* 'A' at the Royal Air Force
College, Cranwell. *(Jim Simpson Collection)*

Below: Hawker Hunter F.1 *WT660* guards the gate at RAF
Carlisle wearing the maintenance airframe serial number 7421M.
(Jim Simpson Collection)

Opposite: Westland Whirlwind HAR.10 *XD184* wearing the
Scorpion badge of 84 Squadron at RAF Akrotiri, Cyprus.
(Jim Simpson Collection)

Below: Immaculate Westland Wessex HAS.1 *XS868* outside Royal
Navy Aircraft Yard Fleetlands in Hampshire. *(Jim Simpson Collection)*

Overleaf: Avro Vulcan B.2 *XM571* was converted to a K.2 and now guards the gate at RAF Gibraltar wearing the badge of 50 Squadron. *(Jim Simpson Collection)*

Opposite: Fairey Gannet T.5 *XG882*, a previous occupant of the fire dump, shares the gate at Lossiemouth with Shackleton *WL738*. It has been restored in the markings of LM: 771 of 849 Squadron Headquarters Flight. *(Jim Simpson Collection)*

Below: Avro Shackleton MR.2c *WL738* in the markings of '38' of 8 Squadron at Lossiemouth. *(Jim Simpson Collection)*

Opposite: Supermarine Spitfire PR.19 *PM651* preserved at RAF
Benson. *(Author's Collection)*

Below: Supermarine Spitfire F.21 *LA226*, one of two Spitfires
outside the RAF Memorial Chapel at Biggin Hill in Kent.
(Author's Collection)

Opposite: Handley Page Hastings T.5 *TG503* at RAF Gatow in West Berlin. Preserved as a monument to the Berlin Air Lift. *(Jim Simpson Collection)*

Below: Immobilised by the Special Air Service raid on Pebble Island in May 1982 and then moved to RAF Stanley to become the gate guard, Argentinian Air Force Pucara *A-529* has now been passed to the Falklands Islands Government for eventual display in a museum at Port Stanley. *(Jim Simpson Collection)*

Opposite: Blackburn Beverley C.1 *XH124* on display outside the RAF Museum at Hendon, still wearing the desert camouflage of 84 Squadron. *(Jim Simpson Collection)*

Below: De Havilland Vampire T.11 *WZ576* belonging to 2192 Squadron Air Training Corps is kept at the Appleby Grammar School near Penrith in Cumbria. *(Jim Simpson Collection)*

Overleaf: Supermarine Spitfire Vb *BM597* on the gate at Church Fenton in 609 Squadron colour scheme. *(Jim Simpson Collection)*

Opposite: On the gate at RAF Honington in Suffolk, Blackburn Buccaneer S.2 *XK526* is also allocated the maintenance airframe serial 8648M. *(Jim Simpson Collection)*

Below: The third gate guard at Lossiemouth, Blackburn Buccaneer S.1 *XK532* in the markings of 632:LM of 736 Squadron, Royal Navy. *(Jim Simpson Collection)*

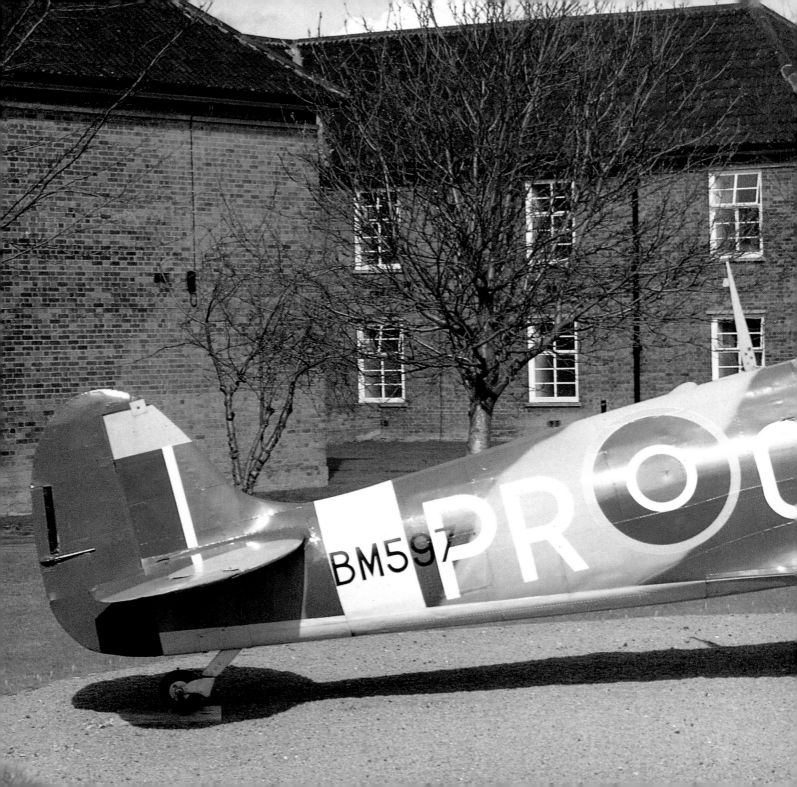

Opposite: Republic F-105D Thunderchief *10217* is really *61-0188* and has recently been moved from Luke AFB to Langley AFB in Virginia. *(Graham Robson)*

Below: Percival Provost T.1 *XF545* guards the gate at Linton-on-Ouse in North Yorkshire. *(Jim Simpson Collection)*

Opposite: Republic F-105D Thunderchief *61-0073* wearing an incorrectly applied serial number, at Hampton Aerospace Park, near Langley AFB in Virginia. *(Author's Collection)*

Below: Wearing another variation on the Thunderbirds Display Team colours, Republic F-84F Thunderstreak *6779* is one of the gate guards at Luke AFB in Arizona. Its correct serial number is *52-6782*. *(Graham Robson)*

Opposite: Republic F-84F Thunderstreak *0-28837* of the Virginia Air National Guard on display in Richmond, Virginia. *(Chris Allen)*

Below: Republic F-105D Thunderchief *61-355* 'DM' one of the gate guards at Davis-Monthan AFB in Arizona, is actually *61-0159*. *(Jim Simpson Collection)*

Opposite: Republic F-84F Thunderstreak *52-7021*, displayed as
'7021' in the colours of the Thunderbirds Display Team, at
Mansfield Air National Guard Base in Ohio. *(Chris Allen)*

Below: Lockheed F-104C Starfighter *56-0919* on display at
Tyndall AFB in Florida. *(Graham Robson)*

Opposite: One of half a dozen aircraft on display at George AFB in California, Lockheed F-104C Starfighter *56-0934* wears the serial number *62-320*. *(Chris Allen)*

Below left: North American F-100D Super Sabre *54-2151*, another of the aircraft on display at Sheppard AFB in Texas. *(Chris Allen)*

Bottom left: Connecticut Air Guard North American F-100D Super Sabre *55-3805* at Bradley International Airport. *(Chris Allen)*

Opposite: A relatively new gate guard, Convair F-102A Delta Dart *56-1134* outside the entrance to the Arizona Air Guard unit at Tucson Airport. *(Bob Ogden)*

Below: One of 47 McDonnell F-101C Voodoos built, *56-0009* makes an impressive display at Sheppard AFB in Texas. *(Chris Allen)*

Opposite: Vought A-7A Corsair II *152650* guarding the gate at
Cecil Field Naval Air Station, wearing the markings of USS
Independence AE: 301. *(Graham Robson)*

Below: Wearing the serial number *00912*, Lockheed F-104C
Starfighter *56-0912* is preserved at Sheppard AFB in Texas.
(Chris Allen)

Opposite: A nice balancing act performed by Convair F-102A
Delta Dart *56-1114* outside Luke AFB, near Phoenix, Arizona.
(Graham Robson)

Below: Douglas A-4C Skyhawk *147727* on display at Porterville in
the markings of AH: 400 of VA-164 from the USS *Oriskany*.
(Author's Collection)

Opposite: One of the attractions at the Oklahoma City State Fairgrounds, Boeing B-52F Stratofortress *57-0038* is an impressive sight. *(Chris Allen)*

Below left: Boeing B-52D Stratofortress *55-0063*, one of the residents of the Southwest Aerospace Museum, adjacent to Carswell Air Force Base in Texas. *(Chris Allen)*

Bottom left: Boeing B-47E Stratojet *53-2385* preserved at Plattsburgh AFB, New York. *(Author's Collection)*

Opposite: On a plinth adorned with the badge of the 82nd Flying Training Wing, North American F-86E Sabre *51-9263* wearing the serial number *52-2844*, guards the gate at Williams AFB in Arizona. *(Chris Allen)*

Below: Rare North American MF-1C Fury *141376* in the markings of Marines fighter squadron VMF-333, on display at Beaufort Marine Corps Air Station, South Carolina. *(Author's Collection)*

Opposite: Lockheed P-38L Lightning *44-27183,* preserved near the gate at McGuire AFB, New Jersey. *(Chris Allen)*

Bottom: Colourful North American F-86A Sabre *49-1272* at Fresno, California, wearing the badge of the 194th Fighter Interceptor Squadron, California Air National Guard. *(Bob Ogden)*

Opposite: North American T-28B Trojan *138353*, wearing the serial number *8675309*, off Highway 87 at Milton, Florida, on the road to Whiting Field Naval Air Station. *(Graham Robson)*

Below left: Cessna GYA-37A Dragonfly *62-5950* at Sheppard AFB, Texas. *(Chris Allen)*

Bottom left: Lockheed T-33A Shooting Star *51-9157* at Sheppard AFB, Texas. *(Chris Allen)*

Opposite: One of two Republic XF-84H Thunderstreaks modified as an Allison XT40 Turbo-prop test-bed, *51-17059* is on display at Kern County Airport, Bakersfield, California. *(Chris Allen)*

Below: McDonnell Douglas F-4N Phantom II *153019* wearing locally-applied squadron markings at Key West Naval Air Station, Florida. *(Graham Robson)*

Opposite: North American P-51D Mustang *44-73972* preserved at Fresno, California and wearing the badge of the 194th Fighter Interceptor Squadron, California Air National Guard. *(Chris Allen)*

Below left: Sikorsky UH-34D Seahorse *150213* in Marines markings at Lowry Technical Training Centre on Lowry AFB in Colorado. *(Jim Simpson Collection)*

Bottom left: Rare North American F-82E Twin Mustang *46-0262* on display at the Centre Parade Ground at Lackland AFB in Texas. *(Chris Allen)*

Opposite: Wearing the serial number *51-598,* former Navy Douglas A-1E Skyraider *132598* is on display with other aircraft used by various Special Operations Squadrons, at Hurlburt Field in Florida. *(Graham Robson)*

Below: The first Lockheed VC-140B Jetstar to be put on display, *61-2488* is preserved at Robins AFB in Georgia. *(Author's Collection)*

Opposite: One of 82 Boeing KC-97G Stratotankers converted to KC-97Ls with two jets pods on underwing pylons, *53-0282* is preserved at Dyess AFB in Texas. *(Chris Allen)*

Below left: Northrop F-89J Scorpion *54-8422* is preserved at Tyndall AFB in Florida. *(Graham Robson)*

Bottom left: One of two prototype Lockheed YF-94A Starfires converted from early production TF-80Cs, *48-0356* is also on show at Truemper Street on Lackland AFB in Texas. *(Author's Collection)*

Opposite: Grumman F-11A Tiger, with no visible serial number, at New Orleans Naval Air Station in Louisiana. *(Author's Collection)*

Bottom: Vought F-8H Crusader *148693* in the markings of Marines Fighter Squadron (All-Weather) VMF (AW) 112 at Dallas Naval Air Station in Texas. *(Author's Collection)*

Opposite: Resplendent in Blue Angels aerobatic display team colours, a Navy Grumman F-11A Tiger guards the gate at El Centro Naval Air Facility in California. *(Chris Allen)*

Below: Republic P-47N Thunderbolt *44-89348* is only one of many aircraft on display on the Centre Parade Ground at Lackland AFB in Texas. *(Chris Allen)*

Opposite: Douglas C-117D Skytrooper *17191* on the gate of the USAF base at Keflavik in Iceland. *(Jim Simpson Collection)*

Below left: No longer required as an instructional airframe, Convair GT-29A *49-1934* is on display at Sheppard AFB in Texas. *(Author's Collection)*

Bottom left: Convair VT-29B *51-5172* in Military Airlift Command markings at Lackland AFB in Texas. *(Author's Collection)*

Overleaf: One of the many aircraft in the Castle AFB museum in California, Boeing WB-50D Superfortress *49-0351* wears the noseart 'Flight of the Phoenix'. *(Chris Allen)*

Opposite: One of almost 4,400 North American B-25J Mitchells produced during the Second World War, *44-86880* is preserved at Reese AFB in Texas. *(Bob Ogden)*

Below: General Dynamics GF-111A *63-9773* at Sheppard AFB in Texas wearing the 'CC' fin code of the 27th Tactical Fighter Wing. *(Chris Allen)*

Opposite: Lockheed SP-2E Neptune *128392* is preserved at Brunswick Naval Air Station in Maine, wearing the markings LH:1 of Navy Patrol Squadron VP-21. *(Chris Allen)*

Below: Black Lockheed U-2C spyplane *56-6714* of the 9th Strategic Reconnaissance Wing, preserved at Beale AFB in California. *(Jim Simpson Collection)*

Opposite: Another resident at Lackland AFB in Texas, Douglas B-26C Invader *44-35918*. (Author's Collection)

Below: Boeing B-17G Flying Fortress *43-38635* 'Virgins Delight' a part of the Castle AFB museum collection. (Author's Collection)

Overleaf: Northrop T-38A Talon *61-0858* on display at Sheppard AFB in Texas. *(Chris Allen)*

Opposite: One of the two Northrop YA-9A prototypes, *71-1367* is now on display at Castle AFB in California. *(Author's Collection)*

Below: North American B-45C Tornado *48-0010* is on display outside the USAF Museum at Wright-Patterson AFB in Ohio. *(Author's Collection)*

Below: Immaculate Grumman HU-16B Albatross *51-5303* in Air Rescue Service markings at Lackland AFB in Texas. *(Chris Allen)*